Paper Chase

Also by Maureen Mitson and published by Ginninderra Press
Jumping the Cracks
Take Time… (Pocket Poets)
Insulae (Pocket Places)

Maureen Mitson

Paper Chase

Paper Chase
ISBN 978 1 74027 730 3
Copyright © text Maureen Mitson 2012

First published 2012
Reprinted 2015

Ginninderra Press
PO Box 3461 Port Adelaide 5015
www.ginninderrapress.com.au

Preface

This has to be a work of fiction as its veracity cannot be proved due to the span of time. However, many of the letters quoted on these pages are as they appear on file. The writers of the correspondence, when named, are all long since deceased. The personalities I have attributed to them are based on the content of their letters, their circumstances and attitudes then prevailing.

I have referred to certain actual incidents which illustrate the trials, hazards, humour and resourcefulness that were a feature of the life in those times and those places. Any errors in dates or timing are mine alone.

Prologue

It all started many months ago. The postman had hidden a parcel behind the potted Kentia palm on my veranda. It was a bit battered, tied around with a network of brown twine, covered in brown paper that was frayed at three corners and with a tear that had just missed a patchwork of foreign postage stamps. The postmark was Kirkcudbrightshire, Scotland.

Snows, icy lochs and grey-stone buildings came wistfully to my mind's eye. Nowhere could have been more distant from me that day, geographically and metaphorically. Our daytime temperature was nudging forty degrees centigrade, not unusual for our Australian summer, the heat aggravated by a horrendous drive home in erratic traffic. My air-conditioned house was an eagerly anticipated haven; the surprise parcel a welcome lift to my spirits. Curiosity mounting, I hurried indoors to give the parcel my full attention.

In retrospect, had I known then what a circuitous and at times frustrating trail through miles and time it would lead me, would I have been so eager to investigate its contents? I have frequently asked myself that question since and I still, many months later, don't know the answer. But I digress. Let me take you back to that summer's evening, as I unwrapped the parcel indoors.

***

The wrapping was certainly not 'post office approved'; I was surprised the parcel hadn't fallen apart en route. Inside was a shabby cardboard shoebox. I dropped to my knees among the twine and brown paper and carefully lifted the lid. A hint of perfume, a dusty trace of – possibly old – roses prompted a sneeze. Tightly wedged within were old papers, envelopes and sepia photographs…but lying on the top was a crisp blue sheet of airmail writing paper.

> Dear Maureen, knowing of your interest in the family history, I wondered if these would be useful to you. Frank.

I settled back on my heels, eyes closed, and foraged among distant memories. Frank? Frank, yes, he was a cousin of my mother's. And still living. This old man – he must be very old – had thought of me, half a world away.

As for family history, I've always been more concerned with the present and the future, concerned for the happiness of my own intimates, children and grandchildren. Distant relatives half a world away might have featured in my mother's life, not so much in mine. As for useful, what did he expect me to do with whatever information or documentation he'd sent?

Mildly curious, I riffled lightly through the contents of the old box. As I did so, I became increasingly apologetic for not keeping in contact with those distant family members. As I asked myself why, my curiosity – if that was the right word – intensified. Old notebooks with water-weave card covers and their pages turning yellow with age, letters, carefully folded, some in soiled envelopes with the stamps torn off the corners; all were stacked in a semi-ordered fashion in the box. Single pages with tattered edges, cracked along the fold lines, were loosely scattered between the notebooks and projecting from them.

I picked up a fat, faded leather-bound notebook with 'Journal' embossed on the cover. A diary…! Inside the cover was written 'This is the private property of Mary Ellen Kerr'.

I sat back. This was the grandmother who died, not only before I was born but before my parents married; my mother's mother. Mum had spoken little of her; she was quite the stranger to me. I turned the diary over, on its back cover an address in Longtown, Cumberland. On the first page was written in the same careful hand, apparently with a split nib pen,

The 8th day of January 1910.

That was more than a century ago! My inquisitiveness mounted as I read on…

Dear Journal, Is that how I should begin? Today is my birthday and I am 22 years old, quite the spinster. I have not been in the way of writing down my thoughts, which are even now in such a quiver because of this eventful day. Until now, mine has been a very ordinary life. Firstly, Father told me after breakfast that he has had some correspondence with Uncle Samual in Edinburgh (in the Procurator Fiscal's Office) and he has obtained an appointment for me with the Proctor of the University. Providing I am accepted, Father will pay for me to attend University! You are yourself a gift from him, for he considers that I should be able to write as well as to read of daily events! Also events today of a more sombre kind. The King is ill. I mentioned that he was an old man anyway and King George might bring fresher ideas to the throne and Mam cut me off, she was furious. I am certain she has never recognised our sovereign family (whom she refers to as the Hanoverians) as Rulers of Scotland. Dear Mam, she betrays her highland blood at times! Oh dear, DEAR Journal, I am away to 'Auld Reekie' to visit with Uncle Samual before very long and to meet with the Proctor. On this birthday my real life begins!

The impact was almost physical. Spinster? Quaint old term. Old King? Samual with an 'a'? I flicked through the journal's densely written pages. There were some little sketches on a few of them; they looked like designs for carving.

I selected an envelope from the pack and opened it slowly. That faint, flowery, dusty perfume arose again; with it, strangely, suddenly, a sense of unease, as if I was being watched, being found out at some indiscretion like once when I raided my mother's handbag.

Even at the thought, a photograph fell from between a fold of paper. It was a sepia print, square and torn round the edges, with a studio's insignia embossed on the bottom corner. The subject, a young woman, was standing against a wooden chair – a studio prop, at a guess. Her skirt was ankle length, her long-line jacket tailored with a neat collar. Below a shallow, wide-brimmed hat, a friendly, inquisitive expression was breaking into a smile. I stared back, transfixed. There was an undeniable family likeness. Was this a photograph of the Mary Ellen of the journal? An inscription on its reverse confirmed it was. This was my grandmother, because in the same beautifully structured script of that journal entry was written 'for Edna, with love from Mam'. Edna was my mum, who died too many years ago.

Replacing the photograph in its cover, I picked another envelope from the other end of the little shoebox. It was a letter written in a faded pencil; the writing firm at the start but progressively less well formed as if the writer was growing tired, or weak. A date was at the head of the page, 'August 21st, 1935', and the signature, 'Affectionately yours, Mam.'

I realised I'd been holding my breath and exhaled softly. If this letter had belonged to my mother, why had it come to me from Scotland and not been left here with all her other possessions?

My normally rational mind was racing. I laid the box down, sat back and closed my eyes. The stifling heat of the day, the fumes and chaos of peak-hour traffic, even my headache, had long ago receded to the fringe of my consciousness. I was cocooned in a time warp with a confusion of emotions and others' spoken memories. I had released the cool breath of Scotland into my living room. Despite my previous lack of interest in past family histories, the fragile scribblings in my hand and on my lap were drawing me to another place in another time and to another's life. I was filled with a strange and gentle assurance that not only was it acceptable to the writer, or writers, that I should read their secrets; they truly wanted me to do so.

1

Later that evening, chores rapidly dispensed, I renewed my wine and sat down by the little shoebox. My earlier riffle had revealed the envelopes, papers and things to be in a rough date order so I returned them carefully to the box, the better to map the events. Initial impressions indicated that most seemed to be directly or indirectly about Mary Ellen and her life, and touching on others only where they touched on her. I knew very little about her; my mother had never been very talkative about her mother, or any past family members. How fascinating, intriguing, engaging; how stimulating, provocative, controversial, challenging, were her activities, her goals?

I reached for the diary, or journal as she called it, that I had selected earlier. Some pages were written in a faded pencil, but for the most part, the entries were in that faded purple-shiny ink, obviously written with a split nib. Most were dated. I was intrigued, fascinated, but this would be no quick fix; the contents of the box would take me days to work through, weeks even. I was going to have to be patient.

Frank must have sorted them for me. I determined to write and thank him. He must be so old now, bless him, well into his nineties, and the events I will read about – and the people – are probably right up front in his memory, as if they were together only a few years ago. I would need to dig deep into mine. I should be able to recognise names, but it would be good to get to know them again, to renew my links with family, if only vicariously.

Sipping and thinking, I tried to recall what I knew of my grandmother, this Mary Ellen Kerr. I remembered my mother telling me of her birthday, all the eights, 1888, on 8 January. My own birthday was the 18th, and in modern parlance Mary Ellen and I shared a star sign – Capricorn. So, she was born at home, in what is now Longtown in Cumberland and was once known as Langtoon of the Scottish side of the border – the area euphemistically labelled the Debateable Lands.

What else did I know of the family? Very little. A lovely place name, Ecclefechan, came to mind. It was near Locherbie in Dumfrieshire, south-western Scotland, and one of her parents came from there and the other from Lochmaben, just 'up the road'. I think it was my father who volunteered this rare snippet of information one Sunday teatime when we were all commiserating about the dreadful bombing of the plane over Locherbie. Mary was the eldest of three daughters, the others being Eliza and Annette. There was a brother, called Thomas after his father. To her parents, particularly to her father, a master joiner and cabinetmaker with his own business and a fine reputation, she seems to have been a trial – a non-conformist, certainly. I knew she had made it to university through her own determination and against some family disapproval. I knew she was a reasonable artist, as I have one of her oils, a moorland scene, painted and signed in 1916. Maybe her flair for such artistry prompted her comments in the next letter from the front end of the box. Most importantly, for me, it asked Wilbert for his help in getting her to university.

***

Monday – at home – [smudged date] 1909

Dear Cousin Wilbert,
    This is a short note to wish you an exceedingly Happy Birthday with lovely gifts. Tom joins with me in sending the greeting, but as you know he is uncommon mean with a pen, one would imagine he could not write! Presently he is in bad books with Pa because he has ruined a piece of mahogany leaf by his carelessness. I feel sorry for Tom, Pa wants him to take on the business but as you and I know, Will, Tom has no feel for the work. He wants to learn about the new motor engines, it's all he wants. I would be so grateful to be recognised for the fine work I do in the shop because I know I

am good at it but though Father welcomes my artistry, when I ask to become a partner in the business, taking Tom's place, he bellows at me, 'it's nae seemly fer a gairl!' Dear cousin, why are we bound by such duties towards ones parents? It now seems I must try for another career, for the one I always preferred, teaching. There will be opposition!

Nett and Liz are so caught up in the preparations for Liza's wedding this month they are like chattering parrots. It's really so demeaning the way they cast aside their intelligence at such times. As you may know, Nett is also walking out; with Wullie Donachy whose Pa has the large stockholding over Lochmaben way. That liaison may also lead to the kirk and Pa is content as he knows the family, coming from there. Pa has already laid by the timber for Nett's dowry suite but it must wait until he finishes Liz's. Mind you, Tom did suggest that Nett could have mine; it was the first one to be completed. He is quite thoughtless at times but he is jealous of my carving. As you know, you and Nett are the same age but if I say a cross word about these preparations or about Nett being not old enough, I am called a mean old spinster by her, because I am the eldest and as yet not spoken for. Ye wouldn't have wanted to marry at eighteen, would you Will? No! So why is it acceptable for a girl? 'Ah weel' as Mam would say. Mind, they are gae happy about Liz's wedding though he's a 'sutherner'. His name is Fred'k Grant and he has great prospects with his work in the Bank. I would much rather be allowed to go to University like you. When d'ye go, Wilbert? When you get there I want you please to enquire for me as to my chances, an unmarried woman of age, with the Triple under my belt I might add, of getting a place. You know, if there are any papers or pamphlets and such like. Will you, Will?

Will, I'm sorry this letter is fair keening, but all things are not as bad as they sound. I'll play the part of maid in waiting at the weddings like I'm expected! My sincere regards to you, to Lucy and to Aunt and Uncle Foss.

Your loving cousin,
Mary Ellen.

***

I thought it interesting that the text was a mix of dialect and correct English. It somehow felt more fluid in its message than some of the carefully worded journal entries. Reading between the lines, was I to infer she enjoyed a friendly relationship with this cousin or, rather, did her natural dialect escape because she was agitated and almost desperate to gain higher education and, eventually, her ambition? Her journals, including the leather-bound one given her on her twenty-second birthday, seemed to indicate a more cohesive and sequential account of her life than random letters allow. Poor Mary Ellen! I empathised with her wish to be individual and independent, and with her frustrations at being hidebound by tradition.

Darkness fell and the gully breezes rattled the shutters. I settled into my cushions, picked up that journal again, and turned to a following page… Closing my eyes, that mysterious perfume – oh, I couldn't place it, more patchouli than apple blossom – emanating from the shoebox, seemed to be a transcendental medium as I visualised her, sitting in some quiet spot and baring her soul to her journal. I sensed I was part of some mysterious cosmic equation; that I was my grandmother, or perhaps she was in me…wondered if she wrote left-handed (left-handedness was a Kerr characteristic)… I could almost feel her, sitting, thinking…

***

Twenty-two years old! Mary Ellen marks her page and closes her diary. Sitting here on the windowsill she can feel the cold draught of air outside of the glass. 8 January 1910. The heavy yellowy-grey skies are promising snow on the morrow. She gathers her skirt around her ankles, hugging her knees to her chin in delight at how everything is working out. To think that Father has finally, finally realised that she is different from her sisters; that she doesn't anguish like her sisters for a husband and her own hearthside.

Well, maybe a hearthside one day, but one that will belong to her as a prosperous and satisfied career woman, only to share with a husband and family if she so chooses.

Mam's calling up the stairs; four o'clock and time for tea. Today it is in her honour and that's why she has been left to her own devices like 'Lady Muck a' Mickle', instead of having to help get it ready. She clambers down from her perch, straightens her hair in her mirror and lifts the latch on her door.

Look at them all gathered at the table! Not Liza and Frederick, of course; they couldn't leave the bank and Liza's expecting her first child in early summer. Father and Tom have even put on clean collars! Father looks up, smiles and bangs his fork on the table and it hums the note, 'For she's a jolly good woman, for she's a jolly good woman, for she's a jolly good woo-oo-man, and sae say all of us!'

Taking her seat, she delights to see the big ham and egg pie from the pantry. It's one of her favourites, and made with Mam's own home-cured gammon. Looking around the cloth she notices a home-made plum brandy, all readied for the toast. This isn't only a birthday, it is a special family occasion, a toast to Mary Ellen and her perceived success; Mary Ellen who is to be allowed to attend university, due to her persistence and her parents' – reluctant – agreement, though with many provisos to ease her mother's heart!

2

I opened my eyes with a start. It had been a long day. I'd slipped into a half sleep and had enacted that little scene in my mind. Obviously my imagination had survived the day! I shook my head to reclaim my own time zone – and reality. Time for a hot coffee. Returning to the box, I picked up the next item in order, a short note. Undated, not addressed to anyone yet not a diary entry, it told of Mary Ellen's sister Annette's resentment at having to undertake extra duties to help their mother in the house.

I recalled a photo from where I'd earlier placed it and others on the upturned lid of the little box – a tiny head shot of two young women with 'Annette and Sarah' inscribed on the back. Its quality reminded me of those multi-school proofs we used to have taken at school – before the digital age – and from which our parents would choose the best. The features were clear enough. Sarah was unknown to me. Annette had a longer nose than Mary Ellen, but the same smiling eyes, and it brought her nearer to me, seeing her image as I read.

The note is undated, and the page is torn at the start, but is apparently written before Mary Ellen goes to Edinburgh; if so, what has happened to Annette's romance mentioned in a previous letter? No answer is found but an indication of tragedy is given in a following screed, written on lined notepaper, as if a part of a letter. It matches no other in the box that I could find…

> …traction engine motor. The horse had been frighted by it and kicked out with vigour and Wullie was in the way. His faither is fair nobbled by it all. Wullie and Nett had sic a future. Mind, Netties only young yet and there are men aplenty waiting to step

into Wullies boots sae Mam tells us. I feel so sad for Nettie but I'm fair glad for mysen…

Poor Annette, those eyes would not have been smiling then. The scrap of a letter seems to be written by Mary Ellen but seems atypical in its use of a strong written dialect. Was this the emotional Mary Ellen as I noted when she was pleading with Wilbert? Or would it have been for Tom, four years later when he was away from home? She would write, I felt, to her brother in the language he favoured. However, it led me to surmise that Annette, either then or in the future, had lost her fiancé and reluctantly taken Mary Ellen's place as her mother's offsider, thus allowing her elder sister to finally leave home. Liza would not have been expected to do other than support her husband, Frederick, the 'sutherner'.

***

So, returning to a more logical sequence, I read…

August 15th 1910

Dear Journal, today I must note another momentous occasion. I have been to Edinburgh this past sennight and staying with Uncle Samual and Aunt Fiona. Three days ago I went with Uncle Samual to meet with the Proctor of the University. He asked me questions for almost two hours about my schooling then spoke to me in Greek. My answers were a little rusty but he seemed satisfied. This, as he explained later was a judge of my intellect rather than an expectation that I necessarily be required to study the language! He spoke of mathematics because I must undertake studies in math. Yes really dear Journal, I am now recognised as a human being and not 'just' a woman! He was also interested in my ambition to be a school teacher rather than to marry. There are fees to be paid and he spoke to Uncle Samual of those, I will ask Pa what they are to be for they must not be more than he can afford now that Tom wants to leave the business. I do have a small sum put by that came from Mam's mother to me. The Proctor concluded by telling me he was personally well satisfied that I am a determined student and that he will recommend me to the Admitting Review Board. He is to write within the next few days. If accepted and before term begins, I am to read some trigonometry and algebra books. I may ask if the Locherbie Minister can take me as a cramming student.

Aunt Fiona is not well, she has a female complaint. Why cannot women be cured easily of these things? One of the reasons is that they will not see a specialist surgeon. Aunt Fiona will not let a man doctor see her person and there are no women doctors around here yet a while. That is one reason women fall sick so readily and stay sick for so long, modesty!

***

The minister of the Reformed Church at Locherbie is mentioned in other papers. There was an account in the shoebox from him to Mary Ellen's father for student fees. Costs appear to have been tenpence a day for tuition and twopence for a hot lunch of soup and bread; total, a shilling. How did Mary Ellen travel there? My Ordnance Survey map indicated a distance of approximately twenty miles. Did she have a pony and cart? Was there a bus service on such a remote route? Or perhaps the minister was a regular caller in Longtown? However, cramming seems to have been an accepted way for a man of the kirk to supplement his living.

I wondered to how many questions I would find answers, as I pursued my paper chase. And just how lengthy was this project going to be. I didn't mind, it was fascinating stuff, but at times frustrating when answers could not be found nor leads able to be pursued! Noting that time had now passed into the early hours of the next morning, I decided to sleep on it. Sleep was certainly calling.

A few busy days and evening meetings followed and, as I was in charge of a couple of complex projects at my own work, Mary Ellen had to take a back seat for a while; a bit frustrating, as I was impatient to resume my paper chase.

One thing I had realised in a less busy moment: somewhere I had a box full of letters – blue aerogrammes for the most part – written to my mother between 1954, when we came to live in Australia, and 1977, when Mum died. Mum was a natural bower bird, threw nothing away and nor could I. Now, if memory served, many of those were written by Mum's Aunt Liz, and some also written to me afterwards, as my great aunt lived until the early eighties, so they would be worth finding and checking out. I'd get on to it as soon as I could and, now that autumn had arrived, longer evenings would be with us before long.

3

September 14th 1910

My Dear Journal, tomorrow I leave on the train to stay with Uncle Samual and attend the Advent Term at Edinburgh University. I will only be an honorary member of the College though as they are all-male Colleges. There seem to be too many restrictions placed on female students. However, I can use the Library and all other services in the day, and living with Aunt Fiona will not be too bad though Mam says her temper gets worse by the day. Mam would say that though, she never had much time for her brother's wifie. Wilbert has told me he will call in often to see how I am faring. He lives in at the college.

Dear Journal, I am going to work hard. For three whole years it will be, I will be nearly twenty six! Quite the schoolmarm! Oh yes, I have had to promise 'not to fraternise with the male students' as a condition of my acceptance. This is really very significant. I intend to gain very good marks, do they think I will follow the gay life of 't'Auld Reekie'? That is something I will leave to the menfolk!

I knew of the old slang name Auld Reekie for Edinburgh – because of its plethora of high smoking chimneys no doubt! So – Mary Ellen started her course at uni. I almost ransacked the box to find some jottings about her time there. Not a note, not a page! Frustrated and quite incredulous, I could not appreciate that three such vital years in her life would rate no – or too little – mention. Nor did anything I could find in the aerogrammes – yes, I'd dug them off the top shelf in the study and had a flip through – throw any light on Liz's sister's university times.

I found a tiny head shot of Mary Ellen dated 5 June 1913 and inscribed 'to George with love from May'. Perhaps George was a fellow student friend? I speculated about her studies; whether she was so laden with them and homework that she couldn't write too often in her journal. That would surely have been about the time of her final exams? Had my twentieth-century university in Adelaide been so less rigorous than hers that I could – and did – have a life outside of study?

I searched the contents of the shoebox in vain hope of finding details about her time at Edinburgh. She must have gone to shows, visited people and even had boyfriends? Or not. It had been a long shot raiding the aerogrammes for that information, but there were other statements about things... I had work to do!

By this time, the evenings had lengthened and autumn rains would come soon. It was pleasant to lock out the chill and the dark and continue my paper chase. The shoebox was becoming less of a curio and more of a determined project, I realised. My family murmured words like 'obsession'. My daughter was curious about her antecedents but involved enough in her own demanding profession and family to check up on developments only intermittently. My husband tolerated my investigations with a commendable degree of understanding and pursued a number of leads on the computer for me. He was becoming increasingly interested in things like inherited personality characteristics, and our daughter's obvious resemblance to her hitherto overlooked great-grandmother.

We both wanted firm facts, data; not speculation and guesswork based on probability at best. I needed to research some comments from family anecdotes which I guessed would impinge on whatever I gleaned from the little box. I delved online to see if any information was available regarding her university term times, names, curricula and so on, but could find nothing much earlier than the Second World War years. However, some reference – albeit after the years of study – was made in this next letter to her sister Liz and brother-in-law Fred (or Frederick as he seems to prefer). Though without a specific date, it mentions the forthcoming Christmas, the Christmas of 1913. Liz was then living in Carlisle, Cumberland, and this letter is significant to me as I had heard of the matter from my mother – one of the few she had confided to me! It tells of Mary's disappointment and frustration at not being granted a full Degree Bachelor.

Dear Liza and Frederick,

Writing from Uncle Samual's to let you know that I have finally won my degree! Or rather it is a Diploma of Education. I am not permitted to receive the Degree Bachelor although I have done the same studies as my male fellow students and gained good average marks. For I am a female, a woman and therefore not entitled to be awarded a Degree Bachelor. Dear Sister, I never thought to question my final qualification throughout the whole time of my study. It did not occur to me that I was not the equal of any other student who had won a place in the course. The Dean knows of my upset and was incredulous that I should feel slighted. He considers I should feel it an achievement to have lasted the time there, being only a woman. Do they think a woman's brain is weaker than a man's? Do not answer that dear Fred'k, I know your opinion, you and I have debated before. But I do feel slighted as I know myself to be the equal of any in my year.

Yet I do know that a woman completing Medicine studies gains a full Degree. It was explained to me that a doctor needs 'gravitas'. Honestly! So teachers of our youth do not?

Now I must seek a post. Mam proclaims herself horrified. I truly believe she thought I would be satisfied now to rest on my laurels and take up my 'ladylike' activities again. Well, dear Liz, you and I know that Nett is by far superior to me in darning, embroidery and potting gooseberries! Much we shall sample at Christmas feasting, no doubt. Can you help, Fred'k? Please, I ask you seriously, if you have any contact in Carlisle of the Education System there whom I could contact? I wish to teach the senior children, you see, and am well qualified to do so. But would you believe the Scottish Authorities will not allow a woman to teach older than Grade 4! Well not at the moment. I have excellent marks in maths and geography and I believe there is shortly some new legislation to be introduced which might be beneficial to my cause.

Dear Fred'k, do see if you can help, I simply cannot return home to become a 'sensible daughter'. I need, need, to teach!
Affectionately,
Yr sister Mary Ellen

I couldn't help wondering how this young woman reacted to her disappointments when in her private moments. Would she 'crack a fruity' – in modern terminology – with private shrieks of frustration and stamping of feet? Or just fling her arms theatrically over a table and weep?

4

Then, after receiving a response from Frank to my letter of thanks to him, I learned – unhappily – why there were so few diary notes about Mary's university life. In my letter I had taken the opportunity of mentioning an apparent lack of jottings about those three or so years and he replied,

> so pleased you don't mind [how could he think I would?[my sending those old papers to you. I only sent the best ones as unfortunately, while they've been in my cellar these past years, a wee mousie has had a good nibble at the corners of some of them and stained some parts. I thought it might have been attracted by the leather you see, but I could not send them to you in Australia in that condition, so I burned them. No point in spreading nasty diseases…

Oh no! A fascinating and vital part of her life gone up in flames! I cried out in my disappointment and frustration; what an incredible lack of…of…understanding. Then, being of a suspicious nature, I asked myself if it were not likely that Frank was also suspicious; of his cousin's frankness, of what stories about the family might be revealed in her jottings? Older people do guard their secrets zealously. Small comfort to understand, but some of those unbidden secrets were just what I was eager to track down!

Armed with the dubious consolation that Mary Ellen was not to blame for the massive gap in her journal writing, I resolved to glean as much detail as possible from what writings were available to me. I rewound again to the British summer of 1914.

Thankful for her brother-in-law's apparent recommendation and intervention, Mary Ellen was allocated a post in June 1914 by the English education authorities. So where had she lived in the last six months or more? I wondered if Annette (Nett) and her husband were still living in Longtown. However, with Liz definitely in her own home, I assumed there would have been room for Mary Ellen and no doubt her father would have welcomed her skills in his workshop for some of the time.

Her ambition to teach in the Scottish system seemed thwarted by legislation. In researching the question, I did uncover isolated cases of such bias which, however, seemed to be balanced with statistics relating to senior mistresses in gainful employment in Scottish schools. She was an anomaly. Poor Mary Ellen. To us twenty-first-centuryites it seems improbable that such narrow-minded sexist attitudes could exist.

Then eventful news: she gains a position. In the same letter we are introduced to World War One.

At Home, June 20/14

Dearest Liz and Fred'k,

I am most grateful for your intervention in enabling me to take the post in Nottingham. The last time I was so far south was when I was twenty-one, and I went to Birmingham to buy book stocks for the Ecclefechan Library. (Do you remember my library, they have an appointed Librarian now and the local Council has taken it over fully. I admit I am proud of that little venture!) On that occasion I saw a group of the WSPU women throwing stones at Mr Herbert Asquith. I admit to a certain satisfaction now I have myself suffered some, lesser, discrimination but in those days I remember I was more shocked! But, High Pavement School has appointed me from September, and I am to visit the Headmaster a fortnight before term starts. His name is Atkins (or Attlee. It is a flowery script and his letters to me are written in green ink, I hope that is not significant). I will need to find board and lodging, of course Mam is scandalised at this. There are lodgings kept for the use of the school staff, I understand. Perhaps I might take Mam on a visit before I begin there, so that she can rest content. She forgets I am no longer a wee gairl. I mind well that she will regard me with some unease until, if ever, I am married and have a man to take care of me. Ah weel etcetera!!

Have you had a letter from Tom at all? I think he enlisted simply to leave behind the woodworking. I have not heard since March and my letters are not returned so I surmise him to be well. Mam and Father are a wee worried but Father has apparently had a letter in which Tom had discovered a longing for the business – the lesser evil, perhaps? I pray he comes home safe from this terrible war and makes Father happy again.

Oh yes, little Nettie is getting betrothed again. To the Minister from Locherbie! Not 'oor Minister' but the one who came to take the Living only last Hogmanay. I mind his name is Herbert. To Mam's delight they are to live in this house – the Lord knows it is big enough and there will be space – and so she will not be losing all her daughters, nor her help aboot the hoos!

Regards to my nephew,

Yr sister, Mary Ellen

Fast forwarding to the second millennium again and an Adelaide early autumn evening; I am learning more of the First World War than I previously knew, which, to my shame, was mainly the Dardanelles Campaign, or Gallipoli as it is generally called. However, as I am trying to keep the information in a chronological order it is interesting to quote from a scribbled note at the end of what seems to be a list of requirements to pack for her new school appointment:

She gives the date – 30 June 1914 – and writes,

an Austrian Duke and Duchess have been assassinated in Sarajevo. The newspapers are clamouring and calling foul!

Then on 5 August, another brief annotation:

Britain is now at war with Germany and apparently it is all the fault of France. Oh dear, whatever does it all mean?

So it was official. Mary Ellen went to Nottingham in England to take up her position at the High Pavement Elementary School in East Kirby and was moving into her new lodgings as World War One became a reality. In a short note – which seems incomplete – from her mother to some other person, it appears her parents are relieved that Mary Ellen

> found the Headmaster to be an intelligent and amenable man and the lodgings to which he directed her to be clean and comfortable if somewhat sparsely furnished.

Of course, Mary Ellen would not be surrounded down south by the beautiful furniture her father and his workmen prided themselves on making in Longtown, not that it would have fitted into the school lodgings! We know that she forfeited her own dowry of furniture made by her father in return for the cost of her university tuition and expenses. Now the furniture – some of whose designs she had carved herself – would go to her sister Annette.

Musing on all this as I sat in my darkening living room, wondering whether the season was late enough to kindle the fire, I couldn't help thinking, as my understanding of Mary Ellen grew letter by letter, session after session, and with every journal entry devoured by me, that she would have considered the transaction a fair swap!

5

One letter written on 20 August 1914 came from her brother Tom, who had joined a British regiment, much to his mother's distress, after seeing a recruiting notice in Carlisle before war was even declared. I suspect his enlistment to have been a means of escaping the family business, as Mary Ellen had intimated to her sister and Frederick.

August 20/14 Somewhere in France

Dear Sister Melon,

    You are the only one I can write to as Faither is sae angered at me leaving and Mam accusing me of being a traitor to Scotland! Do they no' know that this is a 'British' war? I have lost touch with Liza and Nett is too busy at home and under Mam's opinions to write back to me. O Melon, I have a thousand times wished I had not been so strapped by that notice, ye ken the one telling of 'the Scrap of Paper'? It asked us to enlist and said the Powers would guarantee Belgium's safety. Then on the 4th this month we declared war. I wish I hadnae been in sic a rush to get away from the timber shop! Well, it's nae gurt glory sitting on yer backside with the BEF. There's talk the CO (John French) is gae tae push inter Belgium in two or three days. Seems like action is coming m'way. The CO is a bit of a rum'n & there's talk that he's round the bend and that Kitchener's after his blood.

    Will you keep writing to me, Melon, even if I canna reply sae quik? I need the comfort of hame real bad at times, I'd only tell you. Even Dad's preshus timbers would be welcome right now. Let me know how the children are coming alang, I'm really prowd of you.

       My love to all the clan,
          Yr brother, Tom.

(The children referred to must be Mary Ellen's pupils.)

***

Fast forward to the twenty-first century again and me, this woman's granddaughter, a century and half, a world away from the incidents described in these letters reading of them while sitting in my own wee house in the growing chill of autumn, glass of wine in hand. I was musing on Frank's 'burning the nibbled books' and I was still smarting at their loss. Perhaps I should be content to have received what I did receive, but isn't it human nature to want more?

I searched the other letters, hoping for something to tell me how Mary Ellen, at the start, felt about the curriculum, the other teachers, the attitudes of her pupils – as war had just been declared – and of the other teachers towards her; all the personal woman detail. I read through Aunt Liz's letters but obviously, if she had heard at that time from her sister, she wasn't passing on the information to my mother. Admittedly, she had mentioned other snippets, which I intended to pursue, if possible.

I clicked online to see if I could find any indication of any possible school preparation for students who might be concerned about the war and its effect on their parents. Nothing could be gleaned, but then those were the days when children were not expected to think and speak; they were told on a need to know basis. Stoical little people they had to be!

Then I found some loose pages apparently torn from her journal which gave me some insight into her first term – well, at the beginning and the end if not the weeks in between. Ahah! But why were they torn out of a journal and the journal in question not to be found in the box? I suspected Frank had performed more judicious censoring, perhaps avoiding the wee mousies' nibblings, yet allowing these pages to come to me. They were in no way confrontational!

August 31st 1914

Dear Journal. At last I have a purpose in my life. Next week I am to start teaching a class of thirty seven youngsters, boys and girls in Grade 6. They will all be about eleven years of age or so. Initially, I am so instructed, I am to give particular attention to the standard of English, Maths and Geography – this last with no undue emphasis on the current 'fields of battle'. I am on probation for one term and the Headmaster will inform me in the last week whether I am to be re-employed as a permanent teacher. I am making myself some curtains now for my room in the school lodgings. It is a plain room and the few pieces of furniture have not seen a waxing in many a year, but it is clean. There is a list of rules nailed to the door. No tobacco is to be smoked by the tenants when in residence, no strong liquor taken, and no ladies entertained in the rooms. The last one I find a little amusing! Shortly I must down to the dining room for tea. It is really the main hot meal of the day here, not like at home. Tonight we are having fishcakes. I would prefer a piece of real fish!

So that is her class. I found a photograph of the school, rolled tightly and awkward to unravel. The children were in long rows and some obviously on chairs at the back. Girls had huge bows in their hair and wore a uniform smock. Boys were well shorn and younger boys sitting on the floor at the front had smocks on but bigger boys behind had woollen jumpers, knee trousers and collars and a tie! There was a group of teachers seated in the centre, three women and two men, one looking magisterial and with a white beard. A male teacher stood either side of the group. Mary Ellen was not apparent but underneath was proudly inscribed 'High Pavement Elementary School 1914'. But the school was Mary's. Interesting. Could it have been taken before she started there in the September? It was tempting to search further but the hour was late and I had to get to the office early the next morning. It was hard to put down my precious box of secrets but common sense decreed!

***

Resuming my own career efforts on a number of business projects, I neglected Mary Ellen's life for almost a week. Surprisingly, I was finding that my own life was interrupting my forays into Mary Ellen's, not the other way round. No wonder my own daughter was muttering about obsession. I demurred as she herself had been interested in the photographs, then I realised that had been a number of weeks ago. Admittedly, my pursuit of Mary Ellen had instigated my husband's hitherto latent interest in his own family history; he had started pursuing that online.

So it was with less of a guilty feeling that, as autumn nudged into winter, I resumed my paper chase, to realise we had now jumped to the end of Mary Ellen's year from the middle! Lots of dates were simply not recorded. So much was missing! Surely not more burnings, Frank? I decided to stop speculating on that, and concentrate on understanding, appreciating and analysing what information I did have. Aunt Liz's aerogrammes were again subjected to some specific scrutiny yet Mary Ellen's journal entry at the end of the year did answer a few questions.

December 10th 1914

Dear Journal, I am to be a permanent member of the staff and Mr Atkins has informed me that he is most pleased with my work and with my ladylike conduct!!!!!! I am to receive a rise in salary this time next year if I continue to do well. Another 3/- would come in very useful! I am finding myself to be rather lonely at times here now that I am no longer studying. Marking papers does not take up too much of my time. I am hoping to be able to set homework for certain subjects as I believe such home study sets the lessons firmly in place in a student brain, and I could probably devote some more of my evenings to that extra assessment. I'll need permission of course. But I do feel I am making the children take more interest in their work as I relate the theory to the practice. One or two girls seem to admire me for working as a teacher even though I have left home to do it – I think my accent demonstrates my non-Notts origins!

I think I may take up embroidery again and perhaps improve my stitches. I have done some sketching but the paper and charcoal is so expensive. I send home what I have done and like well enough. There is no space to hang them here and of course nothing must hang on the wall in the classroom and make it untidy. I would welcome a kindred spirit to converse with.

Hmm – no ending. Was this the whole entry? And she had time on her hands, so why not keep up with her journals. Then I saw evidence of a wider interest…

It was a batch of leaflets, wrapped around by a piece of faded cotton tape, flyers as we call them now. Intriguing stuff. They were headed 'Women's Social and Political Union' and had a printed ribbon of purple and green ink diagonally across the fronts. I had learned of this Pankhurst organisation, its militancy resulting in some advocates being force-fed in the prisons. One carried a scrawl across the top. 'Thank you Mary for offering to deliver these. Your area for deliveries is…' and that was torn off. I knew of Mary Ellen's belief in their cause and wondered at the extent of her fervour for their, sometime notorious, activities. The flyer she had written on was folded and carefully interleaved in her journal after the last entry.

In the following pages was another single leaflet, a faded orangey-yellow, with the heading 'National Union of Woman's Suffrage Societies'. This seemed to argue for 'less militancy' and urged 'more responsible petitions to local councils and governments' and carried the byline 'Millicent Garrett Fawcett'. Tantalising little snippets, they all made me hungry for more detail. I had long known of, and admired, Catherine Helen Spence, a South Australian who fought for women's equality with the vote and then sought political candidacy in the late nineteenth century. I wondered if Mary Ellen knew of her? Would her scholarly writings have reached the Suffragette movement in Britain? She also was a Scot originally, a link I found intriguing. However, I didn't want to learn statistical stuff from any online research; this was Mary Ellen's tale and I wanted her recounting it to me!

However, despite her strong feelings on female suffrage, I suspect Mary Ellen did not approve of the militant actions of the pre-war Women's Social and Political Union, hence her compromise, delivering leaflets. I remembered her comment in an earlier letter about the attack on the British prime minister in Birmingham in 1913; this shocked her profoundly and the sense of shock seems to have been paramount. She could not bring herself to agree to violence for the cause. I wondered how she managed to back out of whatever level of involvement she had engaged in, then I turned to the next pages after the leaflets. Some had been torn from the diary in between, which was puzzling. Then I read another loose entry. Was this the 'lesser discrimination' she mentioned earlier and was it actually a continuation of the item above? Physically, and contextually, it would fit, yet seemed to be written in quite a hurried way, not in Mary Ellen's usual deliberate script.

> Oh dear, deary me! I decided to offer some of my leaflets to parishioners as they left the church this morning. I stood in the winter rain outside the church porch way, not being a member of this one. I wore the purple and green sash Dora gave me tied around my hat. It was a horrid experience! A few ladies quietly took a copy from me but then a young lad jumped up and tore my hat off and my pins came tumbling out of my hair. I was so embarrassed! And very, very angry! No-one reprimanded the little horror. Then one of the lay preachers came up to me and literally snatched the bundle of leaflets from my hand and yelled at me 'be gone from here you loose woman. This is God's House!' I spoke quietly – but firmly – back to him that I'm sure God created all people to be equal, whereupon he retorted that only men were made in God's image! Another gentleman had picked up my hat, he gave it to me and said – quietly – 'yours is a good cause but this is not the place. Best to go home.' And I did, trying to knot my hair back under my hat as I did so. I was glad to get back into the warm and refresh with a pot of tea. A rather undignified retreat, but I am glad I answered the layman back with some dignity!

Well, I have learned about Dora. Another head shot of 'Mary & Dora' was with the others on the upturned lid. There they were, each with a striped ribbon round their hat. How I wish it was in colour! And this journal entry of Mary's foray into equality was a gratifying insight into the real person; no lack of emotion here, if revealed only to her notebook. I wondered just how much physical energy and organisation she had put into her extracurricular concerns. She had a designated area to deliver her flyers; I wondered how wide, and how and for how long did she demonstrate her feminist beliefs and practices. How I wished I could find other comments describing more fully her own feelings about these issues and what activities she pursued on a regular basis, if any. Yet even her sister, mother's Aunt Liz, stated in an aerogramme to my mother (apparently alluding to my own teenage rebelliousness) 'it is just that she takes after her grandmother', then returning to Mary Ellen, 'she would never have disgraced us, not her family'. So Mary Ellen would only go so far and no further. Shamefully perhaps, I thought that a shame of its own!

My mother had occasionally, over the years, when I'd been tempted to take some easier way in life, an easier course of study or such, instructed me about her mother's determination to succeed in her chosen career. It was calculated to be a spur to my own ambition. Yet now, as I realise the gaps in my knowledge of Mary Ellen, I wonder why my mother was never forthcoming about other aspects of her mother's – and her father's – life together?

The glass ceiling was certainly not in vogue a hundred years ago – well, not in its modern connotation. Though women of my own time are given many opportunities for advancement in their chosen professions, in Mary Ellen's, that was not the case. Some would argue that even now, in this second decade of the second millennium, professional women are still fighting for selection in senior executive roles. I consider Mary Ellen's fight no less fierce because her sights were – arguably – set much lower.

As I continued reading her notes and letters, realising how Mary Ellen, as only a young woman, had to fight for the independence she valued so highly, I felt so close to her as a person that the sense of a cosmic equation renewed itself. She was no longer an anonymous antecedent, but was becoming more real as I read more of her concerns, controversies, and achievements. Despite her pragmatic recording style, I fancied that, occasionally, I could read between the lines to glimpse the 'real' Mary Ellen. Despite weighing up the deficiencies of

The lovers, Mary Ellen Kerr and Lance Sergeant David Peach, sometime in 1915.

Favoured sister and long-lived family correspondent Eliza (Liz).

Mary Ellen the suffragist. 'NUWSS' is inscribed on the reverse.

Mary Ellen and David with daughter Edna, about 1920.

3 Queen's Road.
Kendal.
21 · 8 · 35

My dear Edna,

I can't write much as you know, so be content with a line or two. I expect you would get your dad's letter with postal order. He is coming over on Monday or Tuesday to stay with Grandma so George may as well stay & have another week's holiday if Grandma can do with him. Neil runs wild & he has lost the keys to both back doors so Janie couldn't lock up last night; it's a wonder she slept but then it was Neil. Mae has had to go under the doctor; he is ill.

I can't write you any more so will close with all my love. Affectionately yours, Mam.

Mary Ellen's letter of farewell written shortly before her death.

Artisans stained glass window in Arthuret Church, Longtown, Cumbria, installed in 1970 to honour the Kerr family and acknowledge the Bruce connection. The three figures at the foot are the carpenter (my great-grandfather Thomas Irving Kerr), the architect and the mason.

THIS WINDOW WAS GIVEN TO COMMEMORATE MARJORY BRUCE KERR ALSO THOMAS IRVING KERR AND MARY KERR AND WILLIAM AND MARJORY LITTLE BY WILBERT IRVING KERR AND TOM KERR. 1970.

computer research against first-hand, personal accounts of events, I thought how invaluable a computer would have been for Mary Ellen in her teaching. What of the modern interactive whiteboards so widely used as a teaching tool in classrooms today?

Her parents' allowing her to develop a career was definitely the exception rather than the rule for girls of that era. I learned as the weeks passed and various distant relatives I had written to about the letters responded with their own versions of events at that time – my family referred to them as my own World Wide Web – that less fortunate females were sent to work at the earliest opportunity. However, theirs were jobs, not careers; the worse off financially were directed to low-paid physical jobs in factories and mills. Lack of schooling meant many were illiterate and therefore had no chance of improvement. This would undoubtedly have been a cause close to Mary Ellen's teaching heart. An example from a Mrs Alice Smith who is now very old and was a contemporary of Frank, reads,

> My mother lived in Lancashire and went every day to the local mill and swept up cotton bits near the weaving. She used to get her hands cut to bits and her feet because she had to be bare footed in there. She only got a ha'penny a day and had only a few minutes to eat her apple for lunch. She were lucky her Dad had an apple tree.

And from a James Earl:

> When the sugar beet or the potatoes needed pulling, my dad and his sister had to miss school and spend the days in't fields. Not sure what they were paid, but it weren't much.

These newly contacted correspondents of Mary's were becoming my own pen-and-ink World Wide Web. Their descriptions of family labour and penury reflected, I thought, a period earlier than I was coming to think of as Mary Ellen's. I was becoming more engrossed in the women's struggles, of that pre-voting period, in England. As the Edwardian years in England gave way to those of George V after 1910, women's rights were under more of a spotlight, and education for girls was becoming popular and sought after by parents able to pay a fee. However, after a basic education, many girls' parents eagerly sought positions in service for their daughters as the daughters were housed and fed by others, and also received some remuneration. The entire package took the burden of providing for them off their parents and the bonus was the supposition that the skills learned would serve them well as future housewives and mothers.

Mary Ellen and her sisters were among the fortunate ones. Mary Ellen mentioned that her mother was a fine needlewoman and dressmaker before marriage and her skills had added delicate touches to their home. Having read that, I wondered would it be her mother's fine stitches gracing the beautiful silk and lace christening gown Aunt Liz gave to me for my daughter when I visited years ago? As it came to mind, I ran to retrieve it from its dried lavender and tissue wrappings and marvel – yet again – at its beauty and graceful ageing. It was sewn for Mary Ellen and her sisters and brother and has blessed many of her descendants here in Australia, the last only in 2003. It now has an added preciousness, knowing my own grandmother nestled in its silken folds back in 1888. No longer is it just a precious artefact…

Great-aunt Liz mentioned in one of her aerogrammes to my mother that she was sending to her a fire screen embroidered by Mary Ellen 'as I think her embroidery is too beautiful to be locked away.' We have learned that Mary Ellen and her sisters had been well schooled at home in such activities as embroidery and music – though Mary Ellen didn't like playing the piano – and were all expected to stay at home until they married someone who would keep them in a similar manner! However, unlike the aristocratic families of that time, middle-class girls with initiative were freer to follow careers such as becoming a typewriter or a machinist, governess – and even teacher – without any consideration of losing their properly brought-up status. Thomas Kerr, her father, was successful in his business and proud of his heritage as a descendant of the Border Reivers of legend! In many ways, too, he was forward-looking, being something of a local philanthropist. After his death, his contribution to the area was acknowledged in a coloured glass window, even now in Arthuret Church, Longtown. I visited and saw it for myself some years ago.

So – rewinding again, back to the early years of the twentieth century – it would have been illogical for a man who sponsored boys of ability from the local school to higher education and training to deny his own daughter a similar opportunity. Her father had no sound argument to hinder Mary Ellen and in fact a very good reason, considering his standing in the community, not to do so!

However, I doubt he would have felt so pleased with her progress if he knew of her advocacy for women's rights as mentioned earlier. One of the Equality Newsletters left in the shoebox, with her name scrawled on it by another's hand, makes much of the fact that in New Zealand women were granted the vote in 1893 and in South Australia, 1895! I can imagine Mary Ellen's viewpoint on the topic! I do so wish I could have found a related comment from her.

We know from history that, at the outbreak of the war, the suffragettes led by Mrs Emmaline Pankhurst had agreed to suspend their activities. Many women found a measure of independence in factory work, land work and other employment opportunities deprived of their usual source of male labour by the Forces. This attitudinal change seems to have resonated favourably with Mary Ellen, though she no doubt deeply resented that she would not be entitled to vote until after the Bill was passed and that could only be after Parliament and government ceased being preoccupied by the war. Some scrawled comments on one of the WSPU leaflets reflected her lack of faith in politicians! One such – if I have read it correctly as it was rather faint and despite energetic searching I could not determine a name –

> has no qualifications for excellence of thought or intention. I doubt he can analyse a document to determine an action. He was elected only because of his family and his holdings. His wife is worth six of him and she has no voice…

6

Mary Ellen's journal again lay neglected for some time and there is a significant gap in the letters for the period. That wee mousie had a lot to answer for, in my opinion. Also, despite my earlier lack of interest, I had now, and over recent weeks, become quite absorbed in this distant kinswoman's life, and quite resented putting the little box to one side while I complied with my own salaried career obligations. Some weeks transpired before I was able to resume and, when I did, I recognised a shift in the direction of her lifestyle.

So with a number of notes, letters and journal entries still to go, I decided to let Mary Ellen tell her own story with only intermittent interjections from me if necessary to make a link between events that her sister Liz had pinpointed or hinted at in my other correspondence source.

January 18th 1915.

Dear Journal. Today is bitter cold and the gas in my room smells too much when there is a wind. I took a walk after luncheon down the road out of East Kirby. I felt that some exercise would brighten me a little. I also had Mam and Dad's birthday gift of a crisp white five pound note burning a hole in my pocket. I really want some new oil paints but need some new shoes, among other things. Today, there seemed to be many men in uniform on leave about the streets and they are forward in their approach. I visited again Mrs Honey's Tea and Bun Shoppe in Westminster Walk. I took Wilbert there last November when he visited. (He is a trainee doctor now in hospital.) I ordered myself a pot of tea with a cake, at the reckless expense of 1/6d, and had barely started when this man, not in uniform, asked if I minded if he sat at my table. Well there was a lack of space so I said I did not mind. He made no unwelcome approach to me so I enjoyed my tea. He sat quietly for a long time, as if in thought, looking out of the window so I looked well at him. He had bright red hair, not auburn like mine but the colour some would call carrots. It was very thick and sprang up straight from the top of his head but was neatly trimmed around the neck and ears. He wore a white scarf tucked in his open shirt neck under a black waistcoat from which hung a heavy gold fob. His jacket was of brown tweed, not a Harris I thought, but a good enough weave. Then I realised he was watching my reflection in the window as I looked at him. I blushed and he laughed and we started to talk.

His name is David Peach and he is from Wales. He worked in a coal mine there and now the pit is running into money troubles and the owners are threatening to close despite the war. He said he came to Nottingham to try his luck in a mine hereabouts because there is big trouble on the way and he wanted to get in first. However, he was wondering if he should sign up in a regiment and be a soldier, as the war is not going well for us. I could not venture an opinion, having just met, but I do think too many of our young men are going out there and not coming back.

I have never known a miner before. David is quite clean though perhaps his skin is pale through spending time underground. (Did I really think all miners were perpetually covered in black coal dust? If so, I am shocked at my prejudice.) This David is well enough spoken though and said he had an English and not a Welsh education. From this I surmise he was brought up in this country? I know little of the education in Wales, it is so far away, and am determined to find out some information from the Library. David asked me to go the Gardens and listen to the band next Sunday. I have said I will meet him there.

April 6th 1915

Dear Journal. Time has flown! I have not opened your pages for so long and I had not realised.

Well, a gap but at least an explanation – of a kind…

Much has happened, not least in this terrible war. In my current class of 35 children, twenty-one have lost their fathers to the fighting already, many in Belgium. They are angry, resentful and some misbehave who never did before. I have spoken to the Headmaster and asked that we reserve the caning as it is the last thing some of the little malcontents deserve. Their home lives are strained, housing is short, and rents have to be paid. They need understanding, listening to and explaining how we can help. I feel so sad.

But on a much brighter note, I have the greatest news; David wants me to marry him. Or IS it the greatest news? With the war going on and one thing and another I have to be sure. I think I am but it is much too soon. I have read that men are in a hurry to marry now because they may die overseas. I have always been one to know my mind. We have held hands on our walk and kissed, oh yes Journal, I can tell YOU his kisses thrill me! It might seem to be quick but we have met as much as possible in the last weeks and talked a lot. Also, he has been able to meet me from school a few times to walk me to my lodgings. We have found a small café on the way that provides a refreshing pot of tea and we sometimes stop here and talk for a wee while until he has to leave to get ready for his shift. Consequently, I have learned – as Mam would say – 'a muckle' – about him, and I think it has been reciprocal! We have also met in the town and enjoyed some lovely long walks in the forest near here. I feel that David is a good and decent man (if lacking ambition and I will mention more of that later) – and I am tempted. NO, Journal, I have not answered him yet. I have explained to him why I would like to wait a little longer. He has rented a house with his mother in Kirby-in-Ashfield but I am yet to meet her. I sense he feels she would embarrass me, or be embarrassed by me. He doesn't talk freely about her.

I have not said yea or nay to him, as the matter of my staying in teaching is between us. He wishes to support his wife, so he says. He apparently has no idea how I have worked to become who I am and that is what I meant about him lacking ambition, he seems not to look beyond the next pay packet. I must make him understand my need to do something worthwhile with my life. To him, a woman's role is a home and children and a husband – not in that order! I have ambition for both of us, dear journal, as now Mr Atkins has heard I am stepping out and is curious. Oh I cannot lose any chance of promotion! But is promotion, and the furtherance of my career, to play a part in my life any longer? Not if I do marry David, or so it seems. Unless I can persuade him…

April 8th [very smudged and to the point]

David came round. He has been given a white feather – but he is in a vital industry! He wants us to marry and move away. There is another pit – I cannot pronounce its name. Nor can I leave my pupils and my career. He was quietly very angry. Said he was sorry –oh and a few other really kind things about me – but his duty is clear as he sees it. If we marry he will provide for me and as that is not acceptable he'll do his duty to his country. I begged him not to but he left…I do hope he'll reconsider and come back and we can talk but…I have my duty too! [Inky smudge] But he has been such a good friend.

I could imagine Mary Ellen, at this point, resting her pencil as she tussles with her emotions. Those smudges had to be tears. She was upset, but she had worked so very hard to get to where she was in her career. I felt I would have empathised with her and yet…how strong was her love for this man?

7

The next note, in date order, is a faded letter from her mother, written in that stilted, formal style I am beginning to recognise. Ahah, she advises of brother Tom's wounding in the war, but I suspect the letter's main duty was to express her foreboding should her daughter marry out of her class.

4/5/15 Ecclefechan

My dear daughter,

    I hope by now you have spent your Birthday Money in a pleasurable way. You had not mentioned, but I do hope so. We are most pleased that You are now a Senior Teacher and after nae sae lang. Are you likely to seek a Position with your own Teaching Authority now You have some Experience to show them? I would be aye pleased tae have You teaching Scottish Children.

    We have a letter from Tom, he is wounded and coming Hame. It is early in the war but his lungs are damaged they say. Oh I pray it may be for the duration as they say it may all be over by Christmas. The damage has been done by gas, can ye believe that! He writes that his breathing is gae bad. Annette send her regards, she has twin girls she has called Cynthia and Vera. They have the Dark Auburn Hair like Yours and are as peas in a pod. They plan to take the children to the Fotograffic Saloon in Dumfries so you will have a Picture for Posterity.

    Your Father and I wonder at this Man you speak of who took you to the Music Hall. There is Evil at such places, Mary Ellen; I hope You were proper in Your Behaviour. But his Name, Peach, is not Scots and you have not said he is English. We seek more letters from You and wonder if You would like us to Visit so We can talk. The weather is improving and we shall manage the travel, shall come by Train.

    Affectionately, Yr Father and Mam

Oh, I was so intrigued to know what the parents thought of this man whose name is not Scots – a great disadvantage, according to her mother. They certainly didn't know much about David, so Mary had been very circumspect in her communications to them. I found nothing more written by Mary Ellen, no reference to him, or to their getting together (in modern terminology) for more than a year! I wanted to know if he actually did sign up for a soldier. I wondered if a notebook – or journal – was lost. With such a gap in the sequence of events, of time, a whole year of events, actions, conflicts and compromises was left only to my active speculation and sketchy research.

Obviously her mother when she wrote was unaware that the man, who was apparently a risk to Mary Ellen's virtue, if not her safety, was already off the scene. Of course, her parents eventually learned what happened between David and their daughter despite their hanging out in evil places!

Fast forwarding nearly one hundred years, I know – knew – they married, eventually. Also, my research revealed that David reached the rank of lance sergeant in the Royal Irish Dragoon Guards and that the regiment distinguished itself in Belgium. It was in fact credited with firing the first bullet in the war! However, a letter from the UK Ministry of Defence dated 23 July 1996 regretted that 'a large proportion of the records of soldiers who served during the period 1914–20 were totally destroyed by enemy air action in 1940 and it would seem that those of the above named were among them'. I did find out that the Royal Irish Dragoon Guards were amalgamated as late as 1922 with the Princess Royal (7th) Dragoon Guards and from that date have been called the Fourth/Seventh Dragoon Guards.

However, let's rewind again to 1915–16. Our couple must have been in touch – and reached a compromise of sorts – because they married on 22 April 1916 in an army barracks chapel. The marriage is evidenced by a copy of the certificate of marriage which I found folded up and carefully tucked away in its own envelope, no name, or indicator, on the front. Which army barracks is not specified, though the district is Nottingham. I could appreciate that a measure of secrecy was perhaps understandable considering Mary Ellen's wish to continue her career at High Pavement School and, as her journals were not for wider reading (then!) I decided that another notebook or journal had been lost. Oh how frustrating! What didn't those wee mousies nibble in Frank's cellar?

I had another look at a pair of photographs in a cardboard book-folder, inscribed Mary and David, 1915, that I had put with others on the little box lid. On the left was David, in a uniform greatcoat, peaked hat and spurs. He has a bushy but sharply trimmed moustache above a ready smile. On the right was one of Mary, dressed in a cream or pale-coloured long pleated skirt and long jacket – a very smart combination. She is smiling that secret smile and has her dark hair uncovered but swept back. I wondered who owned the folder. Did they both have one and did David take his to the war?

What was Mary Ellen doing all that time? She obviously resolved the conflict between being a kept woman and a career woman, eventually, but how did she decide? Did she go home for Christmas? Did David have leave? Then, in a notebook – not leather-bound but looking like a school exercise book – an entry of some significance.

June 1st 1916

Dear Journal. Last night the news came through that the Germans have sunk another one of our cruisers, the Queen Mary, during the Battle of Jutland. One of my pupils has a sailor dad on that ship. Oh dear. Other cruisers also were hit and it is rumoured these enemy submarines are the culprits. They skulk beneath the surface and are not seen until too late. Last year they sank Cunard Liner, Lusitania and over 1000 souls were lost. Oh I hate this war. So many of my pupils have lost their fathers and one has lost a mother who drove an ambulance in France! I had a letter from David but it was written three weeks ago from 'somewhere in Belgium'. He has been injured in his leg but says it is healing. I am so worried. I have given my brother to the war, well he is not dead but he was very ill, and one is enough! He will never be his old self and Father talks of him being unable to join him every day with the carpentry, because the wood dust would aggravate his condition. Poor Tom, I do hope he will recover enough to work alongside Father as that is how things should be. And I do so want David home with me, and well!

June 15th 1916

Dear Journal.

   School has broken up early, but we are to return early too. I'm not sure of the reason. Blame it on the war! I am so happy though, David has 4 weeks leave. He wrote from a hospital down in Hampshire and I was only reading his letter from the post as he knocked on the door! I'm so glad it was the end of my school day. He has to visit a hospital once a week though to see how he is progressing. His leg looks strangely twisted, some of the muscle was shot away and he uses a stick to walk until other muscles strengthen. I didn't know he was coming until he hobbled up to the door and knocked like any passing stranger! Well, we spent the weekend in Ecclefechan, joining Father and Mam in her father's house. It has been standing empty for too long. We took the train to Dumfries. The weather is on our side as it seems to brook a beautiful summer up north. Breathing the cool, clean air of the Lowlands is a blessing to our lungs! Father likes David but Mam still is not convinced he is as good as any Scotsman. She is still angry that we did not marry in our own kirk with her able to witness.

   Mam took personal offence when I said I was known as Mrs Mary Peach, not Mrs David Peach. She claimed she had always been proud to carry my father's name and it was my duty to be obedient to my husband!!!!!!. Well so I am proud, but I am not David, nor David's possession. I thought it was because Mam was raised so long ago, but strangely, Liz agrees with her. It is me; I am that anomaly – again! Mam had Nett and Liz there with their children, Frank and the twins Cynthia and Vera. It was a noisy household, very gay, just as Mam likes! Before Saturday tea was over David was calling my sisters Nett and Liz like we all do. Tom was not there, he has been readmitted to the hospital in Carlisle having treatment for the gas in his lungs. It is a shame he cannot be home breathing the good moorland summer air. I'm writing this as David is in the scullery with Father, having a beer I don't doubt! We are to stop off on the return journey to visit Tom it seems. That will please Mam.

8

July 29th 1916

Dear journal, I have a lot to tell you! David and I are now married in my mother's eyes. We received a special blessing in our own kirk. Mam is happy. More happily, David now understands my need to teach – at least while he is still serving in the war – and I will be returning to High Pavement School for the new school year in the first week of September. David was called back to his barracks and it is uncertain if he will be sent back overseas or not as they are concerned about his lungs. Wilbert visited while we were up north and examined David (he is specialising in bones now he says) and confessed he was concerned that if David were sent back to the trenches, even though it is summer, his leg will not fully heal, and a one-legged soldier is no good to anyone!

As for my future, forgot to say I confessed to Mr Atkins on the last day of term I was married. Though he regrets my marriage, he said as far as he is concerned I can still teach at High Pavement Elementary School without any penalty. I think the reason that I can still teach at the school is not only because I am good (I know I am) but also there are so many men lost in the war and teachers are in short supply. George Jordon, the boys' gymnastics teacher tells me my continuing in the post is an unprecedented move. All other women teachers who marry have had to leave in the past, however, as David says, there was no war on then. The Pankhursts are already saying that when the war is over, all the men will want the jobs the women have taken in their absence. Well, we shall wait and see!

We have rented a house in Diamond Street, Kirkby – in Ashfield. It is a little further to get to school but I will manage. The rent is manageable even if I no longer work – depending of course on what work David finds after this war is over!

August 10th 1916

David has been wounded! He was only a week in barracks and they declared him fit for service. I am so worried about him and I don't know how he is hurt and where he is. I received one of those brown forms late yesterday that don't need a stamp informing me that he is in hospital 'somewhere in Belgium'. Not knowing where he is, when I plot the course of the war on the map to the classes at school, is horribly wearing. Today a letter from the Education Authorities informed me that they are appointing a Deputy Principal at our school because of the increased enrolments. The title is not Deputy Headmaster as the deputy will have the supervision of the girls. They ask if I am interested. The position will only be for the duration of this wretched war but oh yes! But what if David is wounded and comes home and needs my full attention? I have written to Liz to ask her advice, she always has her head screwed on.

Here I had a breakthrough! Great-aunt Liz – hereafter I'll call her Aunt Liz for conciseness – had written to my mother about this incident, dropping the information casually as a rider to a statement that I might take up teaching and follow in my grandmother's footsteps. She was confident that it was her urging Mary Ellen to take the promotion even if was only for a short time that secured it for her. I couldn't help but wonder if Mary Ellen knew of her sister's taking the credit? Mary Ellen certainly didn't welcome her advice!

August 20th 1916

Dear Journal. Liz writes that the war will not end soon – due to the inadequacy of the British generals – (I detect Frederick's opinion on that) and I should follow my instincts. What advice is that?

I wrote to David care of the War Office and – they are so quick – just this morning had a reply in that he now concedes the importance, to me, of my success, that I have worked hard for it. He asks only that when he comes home and we start a family, I will then resign to devote my energies to the children. Children? How many does he think we will have? But I will reply tonight and agree, of course. He is still in hospital and it appears he is troubled by his lungs in much the same way Tom has been. Oh I may bristle at the talk of children –plural – but the getting of them is something I do miss! If he gets shore leave because of his gassing (that is what they are calling it – horrible) oh the loss of my independence right now is a small gesture to happiness!

Oh a personal comment. That's more like it, Mary Ellen, letting me in on your personal feelings, not only how others are affected! What a delightful euphemism – 'the getting of them'. Of course, in her days, sex meant what we now refer to as gender. Male and female relationships of nice people only flourished after marriage. But earlier we did learn they kissed. Delightful!

December 12th 1916

Dear journal, David will be home for Christmas, for a whole four weeks again! It seems his leg – his old wound when he was shot through the knee – has been slow to recover due to a suspicion of gangrene earlier on because of the water and constant wetting and miseries of the trenches. The thought is sickening! However, the threat of gangrene has receded but the healing is slow. This is a bloody, bloody war! Sorry journal, I feel so stressed at times. It is not only the worry over David. I find that my new position at school entails such a lot of paper work and interviews with parents, much more than before. Sadly there are fewer fathers to come to the Parent Evenings, it is mostly mothers but I have noticed some grandparents attending. Many of the grandmothers and mothers are so grateful for the sewing classes I have been having in the dinner breaks. One of the boys has become adept at darning his socks and his mother is so pleased. The only way I could encourage the boys was to tell them how their fathers away in the war had to darn their own socks and it is a manly thing to do! One mother asked if I would be interested in her coming to show any girls who may be interested how to knit! I have agreed to that in principle as I feel it would be useful if the girls could at least knit socks for soldiers if not for themselves. We will need sponsors for the materials, though. For my embroidery classes, even the little skeins of silk are now costing 3d, they were only a penny a year ago. I might have to increase my charge for the materials to a penny. It seems I will have to do some thinking over the holidays and plan some sessions other than my embroidery and lace making! Mam may have some ideas.

***

Fast forwarding again. I am certain a vital notebook is missing. Incidents, events, feelings, all must have occurred and were worth recording between August and December. Those months would have been busy ones and I was actually hungry for news of her activities. It was so frustrating to try and fill the gaps when I could only speculate – and maybe calculate. Particularly as my own twenty-first century work was winding down as it did in winter and my evenings were more my own and I needed less preparation for my salaried projects.

***

What did Mary's Mam think about the sewing classes? Did they find a sponsor for their supplies? If so, how did Tom respond to his treatment and did he ever take up a serious role in the business? What of Mary Ellen's David? After this second serious medical complication, would he have been evacuated – a medivac in our twenty-first-century terminology? If so, would David have been able to take on another civilian job? At least I could learn that David was demobilised and not just sent home for Christmas leave. Mary Ellen must have been overjoyed. So why can I not find any record of this monumental event? We have to assume she was over the moon – and she probably was, as the first line in the note below hints at a close relationship, though, obviously, she had to carefully balance her career prospects. Also, it seems he was eventually declared fit enough to take on another job. No doubt he would insist on doing so as, relating to his past comments – he would not be reduced to living off a woman's earnings!

January 8th 1917

My time seems to fly! Today is my 29th birthday – I do not look forward to being 30 next year. David laughs. He is actually younger than I am, being still only 27 till March this year! Wilbert called in last Sunday to see us and he brought me a huge box of chocolates! He was down here for a conference. David would not let him look at his leg; he seems to have some kind of situation over Wilbert. He told me afterwards it's the way Wilbert speaks – well he does speak well, he was taught that way, it is nothing special, but David seems to feel deficient in some way. Wilbert is so happy go lucky too and David says it's because he's always had everything. Ah weel, as Mam would say. It cannot just be a family thing; he gets on well with Mam and Father – perhaps because they have the soft Scots? David did go to a senior school of sorts in his village, run by the Chapel he says. But his parents made him leave to go down the mine at 14. He would have done well, being gifted in math and he helps me plan my lessons. His parents could not afford for him to stay on at school. He does get bitter but then remembers how some of his friends in early school had to go into the mine at age 10. I didn't know that was allowed. He only has his mother left now, which is so sad. Yet I have still only met her the once and he later said she thought I was 'too posh' for him. That is so sad. Just me, and I think that is why he so wants us to have a family. I know it will happen, but I don't know how I will feel if it does. Mam told me that nature will take over and I will feel like a mother when I am ready. I think I prefer children grown rather than as infants. I am lacking in maternal feelings, I am certain.

May 10th 1917

The King and Queen are coming to Nottingham for some occasion and it seems that the best 10 children from each class are to congregate with others in the town centre to line the roadway and wave flags. If they are in landau they will be seen but if they are in motor vehicles what will be the pleasure for the children? Our Lord Mayor will greet them – King George and Queen Mary, not the children – with the other dignitaries. It is a monumentous event! I will be one of the accompanying teachers and I am quite thrilled but David is very scathing. I reminded him that there is a Prince of Wales and he is also called David. He is not impressed. He teases me unmercifully saying that a suffragette like me should not admire such an antiquated institution as a monarchy!

Well, Mary Ellen, where is the report of that event? Surely you recorded it somewhere, as a school exercise perhaps? Yet that last entry was the last for four months, until you heralded what might be a monumental event of your own!

The next note in date sequence was on a page from a school exercise book, a bundle of pages pinned together.

September 4th 1917

Dear Journal, I am sure I am expecting. I am not certain of all the signs but have written to Nett describing what I know. With all her children, she will inform me what I should watch for. My feelings are somewhat mixed, not least because today at a special meeting before the new term starts, Mr Atkins informed the staff he was to enter hospital for an operation. He would need extended convalescence and would be appointing me Principal pro tem, with the agreement of the Authorities! I was delighted and yet I feel angry that the school Bursar will attend to all financial business and any similar business proceedings as a woman is not considered able to negotiate with such highly placed people! Or so I do feel. However, if I am honest, I do find the role of Deputy challenging and a demand on my time and would not really want the financial matters as well to oversee. I am content; the appointment is recognition of my worth as a teacher and I am reconciled as I argue with myself. It is also another unprecedented step and I am the subject of some envy in the staffroom, although most are pleasant enough. Male teachers, who would perhaps have expected to be considered to replace Mr Atkins, are not reticent about voicing their disappointment. With luck, my pregnancy will not be discerned throughout this last term of the year and I will be Principal of a School if only to have a brief reign! If next year, according to my promise, I must leave my work. However, extra money will be very useful and will accrue in the bank if we are careful

December 12th 1917

Journal dear – My last day at High Pavement Elementary School. Mr Atkins came to the school and I spoke with him. He will be returning in his post in January and now he can appoint Joshua Bland who considers himself the appropriate choice – now as well as at the start of the term (!).

David has achieved a position at the pit so our bank account will fatten nicely. Higher money for fewer hours at work! He starts in the second week in January – after my birthday! His new post also means he will spend more time 'up top' in an administration post, thank God. I have worried for his safety many times. We had thought of renting another house with a garden for the baby but will stay here on Diamond Avenue as the rent is enough to find on only one wage. David says there is room for a small vegetable garden at the back – of course I have just allowed the grass to grow! On the 20th though we are going home to Longtown for Christmas as the pit closes for two weeks. I feel so happy!

We can only presume that Christmas with the family was an enjoyable one. Mary Ellen was neglectful of her journal – or those distant wee mousies had another feast. I could find no letters telling about the holiday, presumably because the majority of her regular correspondents were sharing the time with her!

9

Then David returned to work. His changed hours perhaps gave Mary Ellen more time on her hands to write in her journal.

January 10th 1918

Dear Journal. When we returned after Christmas it was to find that next door has changed hands. There are children there now, noisy ones! Their name is Nuttall and he is a chemist working at the chocolate factory in town. I hadn't considered chemistry and chocolate being linked but… I have started collecting recipes of my own for cooking and baking and am writing them all carefully in order. Mam wrote me down some of hers over the Christmas holidays; David does so like her shortbread. I have also started some reading and writing cards to be ready for the baby when it wants to start to read. David says this is a little early but now I have the time, later on I may not!

March 29th 1918

Dear Journal. A Momentous Day! This morning I gave birth to a daughter here at home. She has a thin thatch of fair hair, has a decided 'carrot' tinge, sandy, the midwife called it and dark blue eyes. I thought she would have David's dark brown twinkly ones, never mind. Dr Cottle attended as it was a first one. He said I am too old at 30 to be having a first child, yet told David that at just 29 he is at a perfect age for fatherhood! Double standards always, again and again! But, though I do not find Edna a pretty baby, she is healthy and with healthy lungs according to her Dad. David has lungs on his mind I think. His are not the best, his breathing is so loud at times and fast walking is difficult for him. Also, it's funny but he says he cannot snore! I cannot mind that omission! Mam is down with us for a month's holiday – she always said she would come when I was near my time. The pain was just what Nett had told me to expect but I have already forgotten. We have called her Edna Mary. David now says he will call me May, as the baby has my name. Mam is concerned about David and not so sure time will help his lungs improve. She will keep on so! I have had a letter from Liz indicating that Mam has told her all about David's lungs and other things. I am annoyed. I know we are a family but some things we can decide for ourselves; the family can leave us alone!

Those comments seemed typical of the feisty Mary Ellen who fought for her education and her career. Without a life outside the home, did she find life less interesting, not enough to write about? So it seemed. Being a mother for the first time would have been a challenge, but I wondered if it was enough of one for her.

But oh! I did like that reference to David's twinkly eyes! And the absence of his snoring!

So what did Mary Ellen do in the following five years until their second daughter was born on David's birthday in 1923? Was she content being a full-time wife and mother?

Somehow that does not ring true. After Evelyn's birth, though, with Edna to take to and from school and the baby to care for, her time to engage in extramural pursuits would have been limited, as Evelyn was a sickly baby from the start. Also, according to Aunt Liz, she cried a lot. Perhaps Mary Ellen was so swamped with daily events she had no time to write a journal; perhaps her life had become so run of the mill she had no inspiration to write?

There were no more diary entries in the notebooks. There was a collection of little black and white photographs and one or two of the studio ones, one showing David in his greatcoat and spurs and another with his twinkly eyes above a bushy moustache and a big smile. There were some little dockets for silk embroidery threads – fifty of each colour.

However, I did learn a little more of this period in their lives from Aunt Liz's little blue aerogrammes to my mother. The family needed money and Mary Ellen considered teaching again. She even looked into the possibility of a neighbour looking after Evelyn. David then suggested that his mother might come to live with them and take over the task. She was paying rent not far away and had spoken longingly to him of the children. Then Aunt Liz referred to 'a sewing group' that Mary Ellen formed with her neighbours – 'for company', suggested her sister. I suggest it would have been a least a means of occupying herself with matters other than children! I did wonder if this was the reason for the silk embroidery thread dockets.

David had gained part-time employment in the pit offices but, though the money helped with the bills, his headaches worsened. Then a part-page of a letter from her sister Liz, remaining in the box, invited Mary Ellen (in part),

> Little Evelyn would be most amenable company for our own daughter, May, and if you could all catch the train for some time in the summer, that would be most ideal. I do believe, my dear sister, that our clear air and time spent in our garden with a little companion would greatly benefit your little Evelyn's health.

It was Liz who told Mary on that visit of a possible position as postman becoming vacant in Kendal that might suit David. Her Frederick was not without influence but I doubt Liz's personal enthusiasm after learning of her demeaning comments about the position. However, she did concede David's lungs would benefit from the fresh air and Wilbert said his leg would also be strengthened by riding the bicycle. Great-aunt Liz wrote that Mary Ellen had been strangely compliant with the suggestion and wrote to her in reply she 'feels it worth the sacrifice of my independence if both David and Evelyn will benefit'. David had apparently expected opposition. Aunt Liz remembered and had recounted to me on my visit overseas in 1980 'what a noisy house it was for a wee while!' She reported then that Evelyn and little May 'stuck together like peas in a pod'. Then they both contracted measles. Mary Ellen sat with little Evelyn day and night but she died. May recovered. I could not understand why Mary

Ellen had not mentioned this sad event in her journal. Or were those wee mousies again the culprits?

Then on 17 July 1929, Mary Ellen and David had a son and called him George David. The only mention of him as a baby that I could find was a little card celebrating his christening in the parish church. I had to recognise that either the wee mousies had demolished all more recent journals and notes of Mary Ellen's, no doubt the possibly incriminating ones, or she had simply lost interest in writing. From my mother's rare comments, I knew Georgie was a happy child who loved the company of his sisters and other children and delighted to plant lettuces in the little garden at the back of the house they took in Kendal. And Grandma Peach was now living with them to help with the children.

One item left in the little shoebox gave me quite a catch in the throat. Wedged under some of the papers, and almost lost in the cardboard fold at the end of the box, was a little tobacco tin, only about twelve centimetres long. It was a bit scratched, and dented in the middle of the lid. As I opened it, a sweet cloying smell, presumably from the tobacco, rose with it. Some desiccated minute shreds of the tobacco had retained that sweetness and with them was a metal thimble. As I put it on my own finger, I wondered if this had been David's, for when he sewed buttons back on his uniform when in the trenches, or was it Mary Ellen's?

10

Over the best part of a year, I have tried to construct a logical sequence for the life of Mary Ellen Kerr Peach, my grandmother, feminist and career woman. I hope I have brought her as vividly to life as the contents of that old shoebox initially promised and as a lack of one-to-one interaction has allowed.

I have spent hours online, researching teaching conditions of the period, regimental customs and any other factors that may have influenced her – and her family's – everyday lifestyle. I have tried to knit together events and incidents suggested and alluded to – albeit vaguely – by others. Various official certificates confirm her birth, marriage and death and very little between. Learning about more tangible yet less recorded chapters and incidents of her life, discovering about contemporary conditions and knitting Mary Ellen into the scenarios, became absorbing. Perhaps I have transmogrified the woman I wish I could have known into my own perception of self – that cosmic equation again! In the circumstances, does that seem so strange?

I have to admit that the promise of a feisty Mary Ellen becoming entangled in suffragist activities like bolting herself to railings, verbally expressing horrors at the systems she purported to hate by, for instance, writing to newspapers and generally stirring up her society, were not evidenced by much in the way of proof or evidence other than leaflets and a single photograph of a hat with a certain ribbon. She was never arrested or – that I could discover – mentioned in any newspaper report. Sneakily, I remain a little disappointed! Nor had Aunt Liz given away much detailed information in her letters other than suggestions about her suffragism (which horrified Liz), the comment she would never disgrace her family that I referred to earlier, and some mention of David's rather demeaning job as postman.

Then came a reference to Australia! From one of the ancient correspondents in my World Wide Web – earlier referred to – came an intriguing, yet unsettling, piece of information. This Bob Jenners mentioned how David had confided in him about emigrating to Australia when, in June 1925, his predictions of trouble in the coal mining industry came true. Then, in the following year on May Day, the miners were locked out of the pits by their employers. The nine-day General Strike was the consequence in Britain but when the TUC called it off, the miners refused to work. They stayed out from pits all over the country for another six months until sheer starvation sent them back to work. During this time David, who didn't agree with the stop-out and was outspoken in his criticism, was stoned one night as he returned from a meeting. He received serious head injuries from which he never fully recovered. His youngest daughter was still only a toddler at the time. No further mention was made of travelling to Australia.

It was Aunt Liz, and not my own mother, who spoke proudly of Mary Ellen's later achievements when, as Mrs Mary Peach, she gained a teaching position at the elementary school in Kendal after Evelyn's death. I have since considered that final teaching position as possibly the most rewarding for Mary Ellen. She apparently gained an enviable level of autonomy in the role as she was commended for re-writing curricula to ensure girls and boys received the same basic schooling and intellectual stimulation, at least as far as she could engineer it. She re-wrote the general mathematics curriculum to appeal more to the girls, being convinced that girls were as capable at numeracy as boys. In addition, Mary Ellen revisited the success of her Nottingham craft and sewing classes, and was particularly pleased when boys learned darning and knitting of trench-men's socks. When Singer sewing machines, especially the treadle, came into popularity, boys even asked to join the sewing class. One of their first lessons was sewing up seams on new sheets for the cots in the hospital and the boys relished the chance to 'zip up the seams with the treadle pedalling away'; this last colourful snippet from one of Aunt Liz's aerogrammes.

So Mary Ellen re-shaped curriculum to further her ideals of equality for girls and boys in practical ways. It seems she had finally found her teaching niche, combining her talents, skills and principles. I maintain that she may not have made headlines, but she made her mark.

In 1934, Mary Ellen became ill and the reasons for her pain could not be determined. She was forty-five years old when she first sought the advice of her doctor and was told it was to be expected at her age. I find it hard to credit that our feisty Mary Ellen would not have insisted on exploring the matter. This was the woman who had been, years earlier, so critical of her aunt's acceptance of a similar diagnosis. Was she perhaps so involved in her teaching role that she adopted a wait and see attitude until it was too late? Did she consider her own health so unimportant that she argued against her instincts or was she just so involved in her latest equality programme at school that she didn't want any distraction?

I re-read that last letter in the box, the one I had seen a year earlier when I first explored its contents, dated 21 August 1935. Written on lined notepaper with pencil, the writing became more faint and less well constructed towards the end. Mary Ellen was saying goodbye to Edna and Georgie, urging them to be good and to look after their father and each other. Its last line read,

> I can't write you any more so will close with all my love.
> Affectionately yours, Mam.

Mary Ellen Kerr Peach (sometimes called May) died of cancer at five a.m. on 30 August 1935. So many years were left unchallenged. She was only forty-seven years old.

Epilogue

Above everything else, I have come to realise that Mary Ellen Kerr Peach epitomised the young, educated women of her time and place, who sought to shatter the out-dated shibboleths of sexism by simple perseverance. On this side of the world, life was more liberal, and intelligent women in the various states ensured it stayed that way.

Regarding this last, I believe that, had the term glass ceiling been in parlance in Mary Ellen's lifetime, she would have broken through it. I admire her greatly for asserting her individuality and independence, for challenging the male dominance of tertiary awards and, later, higher professional roles in her beloved teaching career.

Not least, on summarising my paper chase, I have realised the value of my vote. I will never again complain of its being compulsory. For women, particularly, whether considered privilege or right, it was hard-won. That men and women now have the power to vote, equally, is due in part to those determined campaigners of the early twentieth century. And my grandmother was one of them!

When I realised I had gleaned as much as I could of Mary Ellen's life and been led down various pathways to vicariously share those experiences, it was with a degree of sadness that I carefully re-stocked that little box with its precious cargo. I have tried to consolidate what I have learned in a form that may interest not only Mary Ellen's other descendants but also all others whose grandmothers and great-grandmothers lived a century ago and struggled against the inhibitions of their time. As I look around at her later progeny within my own family, I realise we do inherit our past, not only in physical appearance, but also with talents, poise, voice and character traits. I feel certain that we all have a Mary Ellen character in our family history; it just needed, in my case, a little shoebox to start me on the trail.

I wish that Mary Ellen and all those other women of her time could have known the career options that today – on both sides of the world – exist for boys and girls equally. I wish also that Mary Ellen could have known that her love of teaching is among talents inherited by her descendants, with four currently engaged in the profession and two of those becoming school principals. As for her fifteen great-great-grandchildren – and still counting – who knows?

I may have replaced the lid on that little shoebox after almost a year of making the acquaintance of my grandmother, if vicariously, but her determination and quiet dignity in raising the literacy and numeracy abilities of disadvantaged children, in arguing for women's rights and equality for all humankind, is her bequest.

Perhaps to name this summation an epilogue is a misnomer because, among her descendants, the story continues…

www.ingramcontent.com/pod-product-compliance
Lightning Source LLC
Chambersburg PA
CBHW062158100526
44589CB00014B/1870